PRESENTED TO

FROM

DATE

Reflections from
A Life God
REWARDS

BRUCE WILKINSON

with DAVID KOPP

Multnomah Gifts™

Multnomah®Publishers *Sisters, Oregon*

Reflections from A Life God Rewards
© 2002 by Exponential, Inc.
published by Multnomah Gifts™, a division of Multnomah® Publishers, Inc.
P.O. Box 1720, Sisters, Oregon 97759

ISBN 1-57673-949-X

Design and photography by Koechel Peterson & Associates, Inc.
Minneapolis, Minnesota

Multnomah Publishers, Inc., has made every effort to provide proper and
accurate source attribution for the poems and quotes used in the book. In
the event of a question regarding any attribution, the publisher welcomes
written documentation supporting correction for subsequent printings.
For material not in the public domain, grateful acknowledgment is given to
the publishers and individuals who have granted permission for use of their
material.

Please see the acknowledgments at the back of the book for complete
attributions for this material.

Scripture quotations are taken from *The Holy Bible*, New King James
Version. Copyright © 1982 by Thomas Nelson, Inc. Used by permission.

Multnomah is a trademark of Multnomah Publishers, Inc., and is registered
in the U.S. Patent and Trademark Office. The colophon is a trademark of
Multnomah Publishers, Inc.

Library of Congress Cataloging-in-Publication Data

Wilkinson, Bruce.
    Reflections from a life God rewards / by Bruce Wilkinson.
        p. cm.
    ISBN 1-57673-949-X
    1. Future life--Christianity. 2. Christian life. 3. Reward
(Theology) I. Title.
BT903 .W56 2002
248.4--dc21
                                            2002013133

Printed in the United States of America
02 03 04 05 06 07 08—10 9 8 7 6 5 4 3 2 1 0

www.multnomahgifts.com

FOR THOSE
who might be wondering today
IF GOD NOTICES OR CARES.

TABLE OF CONTENTS

A Life God Rewards

Keyhole to THE STARS

"Rejoice in that day and leap
for joy! For indeed your
reward is great in heaven."
JESUS

[LUKE 6:23]

WHAT IF I TOLD YOU...

that the small choices you make today could change your experience of eternity?

Would you be surprised? Unsettled? Skeptical?

Any change in how we think about our future—even if it improves our prospects beyond all hope—takes courage. Most of us tend to cling to our comfortable assumptions...even when they prevent us from seeing the whole truth.

We're like children peering through a keyhole at the night sky, secure in our tiny piece of heaven with a few shining stars.

But what would happen if someone suddenly threw open the door?

In fact, Someone has.

No one made more shocking statements about the afterlife than Jesus of Nazareth. He seemed to leave His audiences amazed, dumbfounded, and even outraged on a regular basis.

Jesus spoke with calm assurance about the unbreakable link between now and eternity:

> *"Blessed are you when men hate you,*
> *And when they exclude you,*
> *And revile you, and cast out your name as evil,*
> *For the Son of Man's sake.*
> *Rejoice in that day and leap for joy!*
> *For indeed your reward is great in heaven."*
>
> [LUKE 6:22–23]

In two short verses, Jesus reveals that you and I can experience enduring joy, even in the worst of circumstances. Why? Because there is a direct connection between something you do for Him...*and something He will do for you.*

Jesus describes a specific reward in these two short verses.

It is a reward for something you do.

It is a reward for the way you respond to a given situation.

Jesus isn't asking us to enjoy misery on His behalf. It's more than that. He is revealing that the consequences in heaven for certain actions on earth will be so vast and wonderful that simply knowing they're coming—and knowing that they will be "great"—will transform how we live now. Yes, and even create spontaneous outbursts of joy!

Is God, then, actually keeping track of what you do for Him every day?

Could there really be more to heaven than just "getting in"?

In a word, yes.

PREPARE
for the future now

The first reason any of us want to know the future is so we can prepare for it now. When you read that the highway you take to work will be closed for construction next week, you start planning a different route. When you learn that your mother-in-law is coming to visit next Tuesday, you start cleaning.

So if you uncovered the whole truth about your real future, imagine how you might change your activities and priorities immediately.

Your daily life would never look the same again.

In the next few pages, I want to show you how the harvest you produce for God will directly impact your experience in eternity—and how that truth can change your life for the better.

Beginning today.

Every action of our lives
touches some chord
that will vibrate in eternity.

EDWIN H. CHAPIN

A Life God Rewards

The Dot and
THE LINE

"For the Son of Man will come in the glory of His Father with His angels, and then He will reward each according to his works."

JESUS

[MATTHEW 16:27]

BLINK.

No transition.

No long and narrow bridge.

No cloudy passageway.

No tunnel.

No corridor of light.

No gradual awakening.

No spare moment to reconsider.

And no going back. Ever.

You and I will move from instant to instant. We will inhale on earth and exhale in eternity. And then...what?

If you're like most people, you picture eternity somewhat like a West Texas highway—flat, long, monotonous. After death (we tell ourselves), all the big events are over, and some kind of unknown, ethereal existence stretches off into the misty horizon.

Jesus, however, reveals something else entirely. As the only person who has ever come from eternity to earth, then returned to it, Jesus alone knows the whole truth. Because He knows the past, present, *and* future, He can give you a one-of-a-kind perspective.

Just think of it! He can see your present moment—right now, this instant—from a point light years beyond the end of your life. (Who else could do that?) And He can tell you exactly how to prepare for what is to come. He told His disciples:

> *"For the Son of Man will come in the glory*
> *of His Father with His angels,*
> *and then He will reward each according to his works."*
>
> [MATTHEW 16:27]

In His great mercy, Jesus wants people everywhere to understand the unbreakable link between life today and life in eternity.
He didn't want us to worry or wonder about what awaits us on the
other side of our last heartbeat. Instead, He empowered us with the
truth—a truth we can act on today to change our future forever.

UNDERSTAND
the unbreakable link between
LIFE TODAY AND
LIFE IN ETERNITY

In the illustration below, you see a dot and a line. The dot is small and exists in one little place. The line begins in one place, then takes off across the page. Imagine that the line extends off the page and goes on…and on…and on.

● ————————————————————————————————————>

The dot stands for your whole life, from beginning to end, here on earth. For most of us, that's about seventy years. The line represents your life after death in eternity. That's forever and ever.

Jesus' teachings show that what happens inside the dot determines everything that happens on the line. For every choice in the dot, there is a corresponding change on the line of astounding proportions.

That puts things into perspective, doesn't it?

Are you living your life for the dot…or for the line?

For He is pleased to give by His grace a value
to our good works which, in consequence of His promise,
entitles us an eternal reward.

JOHN WESLEY

A Life God Rewards

On That DAY

*"For the Father judges no one,
but has committed all judgment
to the Son, that all should honor
the Son just as they honor the Father."*

JESUS

[JOHN 5:22-23]

PICTURE A FIELD OF WILDFLOWERS...

bright in the Mediterranean sun, nodding in a sleepy
afternoon breeze.

Once this field was the central square of the
Corinth marketplace in southern Greece, a bustling
city of many temples and two busy ports. But all that
remains today are worn slabs of stone, a jumble of
broken columns, and the lonely whisper of the wind
through the wildflowers.

If you explore this area as I have, you'll notice an imposing marble platform that rises above the surrounding ruins.

You'll want to stand there, if only for a moment.

Paul of Tarsus stood in that very place, two millennia ago. And something happened to the apostle there that will help you and me answer some important questions…about the life God rewards.

Paul had been living in Corinth for several months, spreading the news of the gospel at every opportunity, when trouble hit. His enemies dragged him into court and charged him with persuading people "to worship God contrary to the law" [ACTS 18:13].

Scholars believe that the raised marble platform still visible in the ruins is the exact place where the provincial magistrate sat to hear Paul's case. The platform was called the *bema,* the Greek word for judgment seat. People in New Testament times recognized the bema as a place of authority, justice, and reward. Officials at athletic events sat on a bema to ensure that the competitors obeyed the rules and to bestow laurel crowns on the winners.

Paul stood on these stones in Corinth before a magistrate, whose name was Gallio, while his enemies argued for punishment. But when Paul's turn came to defend himself, Gallio stopped the hearing. He had already decided no crime had occurred. Paul was free to go.

Considering the apostle's tumultuous life, the incident at the bema in Corinth seems hardly more than a blip.

But it was more than that. In fact, it was a defining moment.

Three years later, Paul sent a letter back to the church in Corinth. In the image Paul used, he stood before a bema yet again.

Only this time it wasn't in the center of town.

This time it was in heaven.

And what had happened to him at the bema in Corinth, he said, would happen to every follower of Jesus:

> *For we must all appear before the judgment seat [bema]*
> *of Christ, that each one may receive the things done in*
> *the body, according to what he has done, whether good*
> *or bad.*

[2 CORINTHIANS 5:10]

When Paul writes "that each one may receive," he is indicating a reward. And when he says "things done in the body," he is restricting the reward to deeds that happened during life on earth. The bema, then, is the time and place where Jesus will give His followers the accumulated rewards of our work for Him while we were alive.

In an earlier letter to the same church, Paul opted for a different word picture. He visualized a building undergoing a test by fire:

Now if anyone builds on this foundation with gold,
silver, precious stones, wood, hay, straw, each one's work
will become clear; for the Day will declare it,
because it will be revealed by fire.

[1 CORINTHIANS 3:12–13]

These verses clarify the first purpose of events at the bema. It is to *show,* or "to give an account." At a time of accounting after Jesus comes (Paul, like Jesus, calls it "the Day"), all that we have done for God will be plainly and completely apparent.

A second purpose of the bema is to *test* our works:

And the fire will test each one's work, of what sort it is.
If anyone's work which he has built on it endures,
he will receive a reward. If anyone's work is burned,
he will suffer loss; but he himself will be saved,
yet so as through fire.

[VV. 13–15]

WHATEVER

Whatever you did for God will endure—like gold, silver, and precious stones. The rest will burn up like straw. Not a trace will remain, no matter how sensible, enjoyable, or even religious these activities might have seemed while you were alive.

Only after the fire of the bema will we finally know what our life really added up to for eternity.

S DONE FOR GOD

will endure—like gold, silver, and precious stone

Picture two followers of Jesus approaching the bema—one is a high-ranking church leader, the other a street vendor. First one and then the other stands before Jesus. Each in turn sees every action of his life piled high on the altar, then tested by fire.

Which of these two will step into eternity with the most rewards? Beforehand, only God knows. But after the fire, both men will see and know the whole truth. That's why Paul could write:

> *Therefore judge nothing before the time, until the Lord comes, who will both bring to light the hidden things of darkness and reveal the counsels of the hearts. Then each one's praise will come from God.*

[1 CORINTHIANS 4:5]

look past our actions to the
ATTITUDES OF OUR HEARTS

After the fire, we will all see the absolute justice and unfailing kindness of God. And when we do, we will completely agree with the judgments of Jesus and the corresponding reward or loss that follows.

In the final analysis, it only makes sense that it's not just *what* we do for God, but *why* and *how* we do it that will create lasting value.

We need to look past our actions to the attitude of our hearts.

Think of the three tests that follow—all gleaned from the teachings of Jesus—as the gold standard to help us evaluate whether the work we do for God will endure:

1. The test of relationship.

A life God rewards is *not* about performance apart from a relationship with Jesus. "Abide in Me, and I in you," Jesus told His followers. "As the branch cannot bear fruit of itself, unless it abides in the vine, neither can you, unless you abide in Me" [JOHN 15:4].

We must first choose personally to place all our trust in Jesus Christ and draw our spiritual life from Him. Only then can our works for Him begin to add up for His glory and our reward.

2. The test of motive.

What should be our motive? To serve God and bring Him glory. Jesus said, "Take heed that you do not do your charitable deeds before men, to be seen by them. Otherwise you have no reward from your Father in heaven" [MATTHEW 6:1]. Even ordinary actions like eating and drinking can bring God glory [1 CORINTHIANS 10:31]. By contrast, our most "religious" actions are worthless if our motive is to build up our own ego or reputation.

3. The test of love.

True good works are always focused on sincerely trying to improve the well-being of another. Jesus said, "But love your enemies, do good, and lend, hoping for nothing in return; and your reward will be great, and you will be sons of the Most High. For He is kind to the unthankful and evil" [LUKE 6:35].

In his famous sermon on love, Paul pointed out that without love, good deeds will not benefit the doer: "Though I bestow all my goods to feed the poor, and though I give my body to be burned, but have not love, it profits me nothing" [1 CORINTHIANS 13:3–4].

A LIFE GOD REWARDS *is not about performance apart from* JESUS

TESTED

The "tested by fire" passage in 1 Corinthians 3:12–15 ends with a most memorable phrase—"saved, yet so as through fire."

This is the part about our futures that so few seem to have ever grasped: When we stand before the bema of Jesus, *we may suffer loss.*

Loss in heaven? What a startling thought! The idea seems contradictory, for example, that a person could be a true follower of Jesus and yet have only a few good works that remained for reward in eternity. But that is what these passages clearly show.

The apostle John, perhaps the closest of the friends of Jesus, referred to loss of potential reward when he warned:

> *Look to yourselves, that we do not lose those things*
> *we worked for, but that we may receive a full reward.*
>
> [2 JOHN 1:8]

He rules with justice, power, and mercy...
HE WANTS TO REWARD YOU!

Remarkable, isn't it? You could do a work and then lose the reward for it. No wonder John pleaded, "Little children, abide in Him, that when He appears, we may have confidence and not be ashamed before Him at His coming" [1 JOHN 2:28].

Friend, remember that the foremost purpose and promise of the bema is gain, not loss. It is Awards Day, the day of distribution. It will be your final, unforgettable, absolute proof that from the hour you chose Jesus as your Lord and Savior, God has noticed and remembered your every effort for Him and your every suffering on His behalf. The bema is where God wants to finally and forever reveal to you the whole picture of who He is.

He is love.

He is truth.

He rules with justice, power, and mercy…

And He wants to reward you!

God is eager to reward us and does everything
possible to help us lay up rewards.
Let us determine by the grace of God
not to be empty handed when we stand before the bema,
the Judgment Seat of Christ.

THEODORE H. EPP

The Question of
YOUR
LIFE

"Whoever desires to become great among you shall be your servant.... For even the Son of Man did not come to be served, but to serve, and to give His life a ransom for many."

JESUS

[MARK 10:43,45]

WHEN YOU GET THERE...

when the pain and sorrows of earth are already a fading memory...

when you draw your first breath of that fragrant, morning-fresh air...

when you open your eyes to reality beyond all dreams, truth beyond all imagination...

what will your heart desire?

To see your loved ones? Of course.

To run into the arms of Jesus? Yes.

To cry out in wonder and praise to the One who redeemed you and paid the price to bring you to heaven? Yes and yes!

When you and I stand together in His presence—knowing and seeing who Jesus is, and how He has dealt with us—we'll do our best to shake the rafters of heaven with our praise.

But I'm also convinced we will crave something more.

We will be on fire—joyous, consuming, rapturous fire—to serve Him. Worship and praise simply won't be enough. We will want to *do* something for Him.

When you and I love someone with all our hearts, words are wonderful and precious, but we're compelled to go beyond words to action. We long to give, to help, to protect, to serve.

Married men and women sometimes look back in amazement at their memories of courting. A man may drive five hundred miles one way to visit his fiancée at college for one brief but precious day—only to turn around and drive those same five hundred miles back home again. And do it all again the following Friday. Gladly! No sacrifice is too great! No gesture too grand! No inconvenience too bothersome. When you're heart-over-heels in love, words just aren't enough. You're almost bursting—exploding—with the desire to *do* something for that cherished person.

Words weren't enough for God, either. He loved you and every person in His world so much that He did something dramatic— He gave His Son. Jesus said that the greatest expression of love is to do something—"to lay down one's life for his friends" [JOHN 15:13].

But as we will see, *greater opportunity to serve God in heaven is a specific reward for how well we serve Him here with everything He has entrusted to our care.*

the greatest expression of love

TO DO SOMETHING

The Bible often uses the word *steward* to describe a servant who has been charged with managing his master's assets.

Jesus told parables about stewards for an important and specific reason. Jesus would be going away. Later, He would return. And during His absence, the business of His kingdom on earth would be entirely in the hands of His followers.

If you are a follower of Jesus, you are in the same circumstance as the disciples. Like them, you live in the in-between season of great opportunity. You have been given a trust, your Master has not yet returned, and every day you should answer this question:

How will I steward what my Master has placed in my care?

Whether we act intentionally on our commission or not, we are deciding by our actions how we will use our time, talents, energies, and skills.

The Bible uses one word more than any other to describe the conduct of a good steward.

That word is *faithful.*

The two best-known parables of Jesus concerning stewards—the Parable of the Minas and the Parable of the Talents—contain startling truths about the life God rewards.

The Parable of the Minas, found in Luke 19, begins when a nobleman calls ten servants together and gives each one a mina (about three years' wages). The steward's assignment? "Do business till I come" [V. 13]. The master gave an identical amount to each steward, who could multiply it as much as any of the others.

When the nobleman returns, he calls for an accounting. The first servant reports a tenfold increase on his investment of his master's mina. The master responds, "Well done, good servant; because you were faithful in a very little, have authority over ten cities" [V. 17].

reward is based on POTENTIAL

When the second servant reports a fivefold return, the master replies, "You also be over five cities" [V. 19]. Yet what is most notable is what the master doesn't say to him. He doesn't say, "Well done," or "good servant," or even "because you were faithful in a very little." The lesser level of commendation shows that the master knew the servant could have done more to multiply his mina.

It's completely different in the second story, the Parable of the Talents [MATTHEW 25:14–30]. This time, three stewards are each given different amounts of money, "to each according to his own ability" [V. 15]. The first steward took his five and doubled it and received commendation from his master:

> *"Well done, good and faithful servant; you have been [were] faithful over a few things, I will make you ruler over many things. Enter into the joy of your lord."*
> [V. 23]

The second steward multiplied his two talents to four and received the same commendation and reward. How could this be true when one presented ten and the other only four? Jesus teaches that a servant's reward is based on his potential, not his total in comparison to another (unlike the minas, where each received the same). Both stewards in this parable doubled what Christ gave them, and both received the same reward. In that way, all of us are equally able to earn rewards.

The third servant in each story simply returns the investment he'd been given, explaining that he kept the valuables safely hidden at home. Imagine that servant's shame when his master calls him "wicked servant," then takes his single mina and gives it to the servant who had earned the most!

Reflecting on these parables of Jesus, let me show you three common misconceptions about stewardship among Christians today and the corresponding truths Jesus wants us to see:

- We think that even though God gave us our gifts and talents, He is not bothered if we don't make the most of every opportunity.

But the truth of the first steward is God expects us to take the resources of our lives and greatly *multiply* them for His kingdom.

- We think that if God does reward us for serving Him, His reward will be a general commendation that will apply to everyone equally and won't change our future opportunities in His kingdom.

But the truth of the second steward is that God will reward our work for Him in *direct proportion* to how much we have multiplied our assets for Him—and His response will have a huge impact on our future.

• We think that if we don't serve God with what He
  has given us, the worst that could happen will be
  no reward.

But the truth of the third steward is that if we do not multiply
what God has placed in our care, we will suffer *loss*—both of the
potential reward we could have earned and of the opportunity to
serve God more fully in eternity with the very gifts He entrusted
to us on earth.

Jesus wants you to clearly grasp how much is at stake for your
eternal future in your choices now. By the quality of your service
now, you are preparing for the depth of your service in heaven.

your choices now affect your
ETERNAL FUTURE

Maybe you find yourself thinking, *I don't have many talents or opportunities, so how can I bring God much return for my life? Does that mean I won't have the chance to serve Him much in eternity?*

Remember the Parable of the Talents? Both the one who had much to invest and the one who had little to invest were commended in precisely the same way for faithful service.

Are you a seamstress or the leader of a nation? A factory worker or a young mother? A village pastor or a builder? Jesus reveals that every disciple has the same opportunity for service now and the same opportunity for great reward later. In fact, your future is as promising and important as the future of the most gifted person in history.

If, with God's help, you use your full potential for Him, He will grant you the privilege and reward of great service to Him forever. And when you stand before Jesus at the bema, He will tell you from His heart, "Well done, good and faithful servant...enter into the joy of your Lord."

He will grant you
PRIVILEGE AND

That joy will be so wild and sweet, so vast and towering, that we may want to ponder it for ten million years or so. Then again, it may thrust us immediately into the farthest galaxies of those bright new heavens…with the desire to serve and serve and serve our Savior and King.

There will be varying degrees of reward in heaven.
That shouldn't surprise us:
There are varying degrees
of giftedness even here on earth.

JOHN MACARTHUR JR.

REWARD

The God Who GIVES BACK

"Do not lay up for yourselves treasures on earth, where moth and rust destroy and where thieves break in and steal; but lay up for yourselves treasures in heaven, where neither moth nor rust destroys and where thieves do not break in and steal."

JESUS

[MATTHEW 6:19-20]

I WAS TAKING A COFFEE BREAK...

at a family conference in Kentucky when nine-year-old Will walked up, stood beside my chair, and asked if I wanted to donate to a missions project.

"What would you use my money for?" I asked.

Will held out a radio. "This radio runs by sun power," he said proudly. "It's for people who live in the jungles. People can listen to this radio to learn things and hear about Jesus."

I decided on the spot to make Will an offer. "Tell you what," I said, "I'll give to your project, but you have to give money, too." On one of his donation cards, I wrote out my proposal:

> *Will,*
>
> *If you give one to five dollars,*
>> *I'll give double what you give.*
>
> *If you give six to ten dollars,*
>> *I'll give triple what you give.*
>
> *If you give eleven to twenty dollars,*
>> *I'll give four times what you give.*

I signed my name and Will read the card. By the time he was finished, his eyes were as big as saucers. Then suddenly his face fell, and he stared at the floor.

"Don't you like my idea?" I asked.

"Yeah," he said, shuffling his feet.

"Well, what are you going to do?"

"Nothing."

"Nothing?"

"I can't," he said. "I already gave everything I had."

I felt a pang in my heart. "You mean you put all your money in your own fund drive?" I asked.

He nodded.

At that moment, I knew what I needed to do. "Actually, Will," I began, "I have a rule that if you give everything you have, I will give everything I have, too."

As it happened, I'd just been to a bank to withdraw a considerable amount of cash for my trip. I reached under the table for my briefcase, pulled out a bank envelope of bills, and handed it to Will.

I'm not sure who was more surprised—Will or me. Now both of us had eyes as big as saucers, but we were both grinning happily, too....

My experience with Will has come to illustrate a truth for me about giving—a truth so surprising it hardly sounds possible: *Whatever I give to God on earth, He will more than give back to me in heaven.*

The faithful servants of Christ
shall not be put off with mere commendation—
all their work and labor of love
shall be rewarded.

MATTHEW HENRY

WHATEVER I GIVE GOD
He will more than give back in heaven.

What did Jesus really teach about money and possessions?

Peter may have first heard it clearly when he listened to Jesus telling a wealthy young man why he should leave his possessions and money to follow Him. He said, "You will have treasure in heaven" [MATTHEW 19:21].

When the man turned down Jesus' offer and left, Peter stepped forward to ask the obvious question:

> *"See, we have left all and followed You.*
> *Therefore what shall we have?"*
>
> [V. 27]

I love the fact that Jesus didn't scold Peter for his question. Or smile indulgently and say, "Peter, Peter, I wasn't speaking *literally* about treasure in heaven." Instead, He gave a most revealing answer. Jesus told Peter that he and the other disciples would rule over the nation of Israel when He set up His kingdom. Then He said that every person who leaves all to follow Him would be repaid a hundredfold [V. 29].

A hundredfold is the equivalent of a 10,000 percent return!

Now you can see that what happened to nine-year-old Will only hints at God's amazing plan to reward every believer who sacrifices treasure on earth to serve Him.

Perhaps Jesus' most familiar teaching on treasure is found in the Sermon on the Mount:

> *"Do not lay up for yourselves treasures on earth, where moth and rust destroy and where thieves break in and steal; but lay up for yourselves treasures in heaven."*
> [MATTHEW 6:19–20]

If you grew up in church like I did, you may have assumed that these verses mean that spiritual pursuits are more important than earthly ones. But Jesus was clearly talking about *actual treasure*—and how you can keep it. He used the identical term to describe real treasure on earth and real treasure in heaven. Why would He have used precisely the same word if He didn't mean precisely the same thing? And why should we assume that the treasure Jesus talked about in heaven is anything less than real, inexpressibly valuable, and desirable beyond telling?

treasure in heaven...
INEXPRESSIBLY VALUABLE
DESIRABLE BEYOND TELLING

You might be asking yourself, "But why would treasure matter to me in heaven?"

I understand the question. But we have to conclude from Jesus' dramatic statements here and elsewhere that our treasure will matter *a lot* to us in eternity!

In God's kingdom, when the sinful pull of greed, envy, and manipulation is absent, we will *enjoy* our treasure, and it will serve a pure and meaningful purpose. As we'll see, our treasure will allow us to serve, to give, to accomplish, and to experience more for Him. Forever.

But there's something very specific we must do, Jesus said, to "transfer" our treasure to heaven.

SERVE
GIVE
ACCOMPLISH
to experience more for Him

I remember years ago, when Darlene Marie and I moved across the country. As we stood in our driveway watching the moving van pull away, it occurred to me that—aside from the bare essentials—the truck contained our most important belongings and personal treasures. Since our plan was to follow later by car, we wouldn't see our possessions again until weeks later, when we arrived at our new home.

That's not a bad picture of the treasure we forward on to heaven. We stay behind with a few essentials, awaiting the journey to our new home. But the real goods—if we intend to keep their value through eternity—must go on ahead.

Think of it as God's moving plan: *To move your treasure to heaven, you have to send it ahead.*

How do we accomplish that? One day, Jesus advised His disciples:

> *"Sell what you have and give alms; provide yourselves money bags which do not grow old, a treasure in the heavens that does not fail, where no thief approaches nor moth destroys."*
>
> [LUKE 12:33]

This verse shows the clear link between an action regarding treasure on earth and the result of that action in heaven. If you "give alms" now, Scripture tells us, you will actually "provide yourselves" with something valuable later—"a treasure in the heavens."

Paul told Timothy to command the well-to-do members of his church to "be rich in good works, ready to give, willing to share, *storing up for themselves a good foundation for the time to come*" [1 TIMOTHY 6:18–19].

Jesus said it even more simply:

> *"Where your treasure is, there your heart will be also."*
>
> [MATTHEW 6:21]

TO MOVE YOUR TREASURE
TO HEAVEN
you have to send it ahead

Do good,
and it will follow of itself without your seeking,
that you will have friends,
find treasures in heaven,
and receive a reward.

MARTIN LUTHER

A Final
PROMISE

"And behold, I am coming quickly,
and My reward is with Me,
to give to every one
according to his work."

JESUS

[REVELATION 22:12]

I'LL NEVER FORGET
THE STORY...

of a missionary couple from Great Britain who had
spent a lifetime serving God in some far corner of the
earth. The century turned. A world war was fought.
After forty years had passed, they wrote their supporters
that they were coming home and sailed for England.

When they laid eyes on their country's coastline for the first time in decades, the man said to his wife, "I wonder if anyone will be here to welcome us home."

As the ship sailed into Plymouth Harbor, the elderly couple stood on the upper deck of the ocean liner, holding hands. Then, to their surprise and pleasure, they saw that throngs of people crowded the dock, pointing in their direction and cheering. A band played. Men held up a banner that read, "Welcome home! We're proud of you!"

The husband was deeply moved. "Isn't this wonderful!" His wife laughed happily, and they decided it was time to go below to collect their luggage.

But as they emerged onto the gangplank, their hearts pounding with anticipation, they were taken aback. The crowd had already started to disperse. Soon it became all too clear what had happened. The huge welcome was not for them, but for a politician returning from some foreign success.

In fact, no one was there to greet them at all.

The husband could hardly contain his disappointment. "After a lifetime of service, you'd think…well, this isn't much of a welcome home."

His wife took his arm. "Come along, sweetheart," she said softly. "This is just England. We're not home yet."

EVERY DAY IS AN OPPORTUNITY
TO DISCOVER
eternal business lurking in ordinary business

I remember when Darlene Marie and I first chose to believe in God's eternal reward and to live for that Day. It dramatically changed our actions and priorities. It reordered how our family handled our money, our time, and our abilities. It added new, obvious urgency to how we tended to unfinished business. We became more grateful, more overwhelmed by the kindness of God.

And we began to live every day for the Rewarder's "Well done."

Since then, we've met hundreds of other men and women who, at Jesus' invitation, have looked into eternity and are now on an outrageous mission—to live for God's pleasure.

They are wealthy businessmen who have told us they "owned" nothing, not even their shoes. They are students who see an adventure for God in every new face, every difficult class and belittling job. They are young mothers who enthusiastically serve a great King, realizing that their most important work for all of eternity might be the little ones sleeping in the nursery or toddling down the hall.

These exuberant pilgrims seem a lot like other people on the surface, but they understand a day's possibilities from a completely different point of view. Every day is a new opportunity to discover what eternal business might be lurking in the ordinary business of being human.

Sure, they are living *in* the dot, but they are living *for* the line. They're making a difference for God on the streets of New Delhi and Manchester and Lagos and Biloxi…

They are already citizens of heaven, and they've sent everything that really matters on ahead.

By God's enabling grace, let's follow in their path.

He is waiting to welcome us!
To those who serve, to those who stand
where Jesus Christ once stood many,
many years ago, He promises a reward.
And we can be sure He will keep His promise.

CHARLES R. SWINDOLL

ACKNOWLEDGMENTS

Theodore H. Epp quote taken from
Present Labor and Future Rewards
by Theodore H. Epp
(Lincoln, Neb., Back to the Bible, 1960), 78, 86.
Used by permission.

John MacArthur Jr. quote taken from
"Bible Questions and Answers,"
GC 70-13, 1992, cassette.
Source: www.biblebb.com/files/macqa/70-13-5.htm.
Used by permission.

Charles R. Swindoll quote from
Improving Your Serve
by Charles R. Swindoll
© 1981 W Publishing Group, Nashville, Tennessee.
All rights reserved.